DON'T BELIEVE EVERYTHING YOU THINK

Don't miss our other titles about emotions:

Up and Down, Round and Round: A Day in the Life of Emotions;

The Bear is Not There: A Book About the Nervous System + Coping Strategies

And sometimes our body's sensations make us think thoughts.

If we have a tummy ache, our brains decide *why* our tummy hurts.
It might decide that we are worried or scared,
but we actually ate something that made us feel kind of sick.

Our thoughts are *powerful*.
They can make emotions bigger or smaller.
They can make us happier or sadder.
They can make us feel like the whole world is against us,
or that we are the luckiest person on earth.

That's why it's important to make sure that our thoughts are telling us the truth, and not making a situation worse for no reason.

But sometimes, we think thoughts that make the *frustrated* emotion bigger and bigger... until all of a sudden it's anger and then it's *rage*.

Soon our feet might start to stomp.
Our heart starts to feel *fast*.

It feels harder to breathe and harder to talk.

When someone tries to talk to us, we can hear their words but they don't really mean anything.

And then *suddenly*, it's like we're riding a train and can't get off.
We start to yell and cry and kick our feet.
We might fall on the ground.

If someone is talking to us, we can't hear them.
It's like the train went in a tunnel.
Nothing we see or hear matters anymore.

When this happens, our brains are sending all kinds of messages to all different parts of our bodies. We aren't in control of our bodies or our brains.

Sometimes it might help to be around a calm grown-up to remind us that we're safe. Sometimes it might help to get a hug.

And sometimes, we just have to wait for it to end.

After the train leaves the tunnel,
our muscles get softer,
our screaming becomes quieter,
and we might feel sad
instead of angry.

When someone talks to us,
we can hear them.

This is a good time to get a hug
and talk about what happened.

No one likes it when their brain or body is out of control.
No one likes going into the tunnel.

The good news is, we can learn to be in charge.
It takes practice, but we can teach our brains to notice
the sensations in our bodies when they *start* to happen,
instead of finding that we're out of control.

ants in my pants

prickling behind my eyes

tight chest

And we can keep our thoughts from going out of control, too. Sometimes our thoughts are telling us the truth about the world.

But other times, our thoughts can get a little twisted, even though they *seem* right — and those thoughts can lead us *straight* into the tunnel.

Here are some examples of twisted thoughts.

"This is all about me."

My friends were whispering, and I <u>know</u> they were talking about me. They looked at me!

MAKING IT PERSONAL

"I know what will happen in the future."

It's raining today and I bet it will rain all week and the field trip will get canceled!

FORTUNE-TELLING

We can teach our brains to have different, untangled thoughts,
which can make us feel a lot happier every day.
Let's pretend we had big plans to play outside today.
We were going to roll around on the grass and lay in the sun.

But when we wake up,
it's raining outside, and now
the grass is wet and soggy.
We might feel very disappointed.
Maybe we feel tingling in our
nose and behind our eyes and
feel like we're going to cry.
Maybe we *do* cry.
Maybe we feel heaviness in our chest.

But we might be able to get creative.
What if we decide to think thoughts that make the feelings get smaller?
What if we choose to make a *new* plan?

We can do this almost every time we get upset.

We can decide to feel our emotions,
name our feelings, question our thoughts, and make a new plan.

I'm <u>mad</u>! I wanted to keep drawing, but now I have to go shopping. Maybe I can bring my drawing...

Sometimes, no matter how hard we try, we end up in that tunnel.
And that's okay —it happens.

Next time, what can we try?

When we learn to manage
our emotions and feelings, we are in charge.
We get to decide how we handle our feelings,
and what decisions we make each day.

Things might not always go our way,
but when we teach our brain and body
to calm down, we can make sure
it doesn't ruin the whole day.

Hi! My name is Sara. Nice to meet you!

I wrote this book (& lots of others!) because I like to draw + help people.

Things I LOVE!
- reading
- Dancing (Badly)
- my family
- nature
- animals
- Quiet time
- candy
- Rainbows

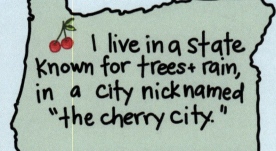

I live in a state known for trees + rain, in a city nicknamed "the cherry city."

I do all my drawings on an iPad with an Apple pencil

I live with my daughter and our two cats, Waffle + Batman. One day, I want a goat, and I want to name him CAULIFLOWER!

Hey Parents!

You don't have to be a superhero to be an *incredible* parent.

There's no shortage of parenting information out there.
But most of us feel like we can barely make it through the day
... let alone thoughtfully develop the skills our kids need.

At Mighty + Bright, we've figured out how to:

- Incorporate emotional + mental wellbeing into your day-to-day life

- Learn a common language with your kids

- Make your parenting life easier

- Reduce meltdowns and underlying anxiety

...with no thick parenting books,
(and no digital parenting courses.)

Find more books like this and tools that'll totally change your family

SCAN THIS USING YOUR PHONE
or visit: mightyandbright.com/emotions

We believe it shouldn't take *more* effort to guide your kids the way you want to guide them.
It just takes a different perspective.